To

_____

From

_____

# 365 DAY BRIGHTENERS™

## to Feed Your Soul at Work

# 365 Day Brighteners™ to Feed Your Soul at Work

Copyright © 2004 DaySpring® Cards, Inc.
Published by Garborg's®, a brand of DaySpring® Cards, Inc.
Siloam Springs, Arkansas
www.dayspring.com

Design by Moe Studio

Scripture quotations are from the following sources: The HOLY BIBLE, NEW INTERNATIONAL VERSION® (NIV)® © 1973, 1978, 1984 by International Bible Society. Used by permission of Zondervan Publishing House. THE MESSAGE © Eugene H. Peterson 1993, 1994, 1995. Used by permission of NavPress Publishing Group. All rights reserved. The Living Bible (TLB) © 1971 by permission of Tyndale House Publishers, Inc., Wheaton, IL. The New Revised Standard Version of the Bible (NRSV) © 1989 Division of Christian Education, National Council of Churches. Used by permission of Zondervan Publishing House. The Holy Bible, New Living Translation (NLT) © 1996 by permission of Tyndale House Publishers, Inc., Wheaton, IL.

ISBN 1-58061-788-3
Printed in China.

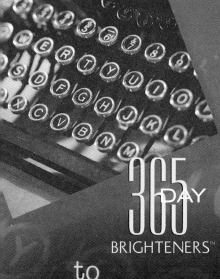

# 365 DAY BRIGHTENERS™

## to Feed Your Soul at Work

GARBORG'S

*because every day is a gift*

If you think you can win,
you can win. Faith is
necessary to victory.

WILLIAM HAZLITT

# JANUARY 1

A business that makes nothing but money is a poor kind of business.

HENRY FORD

# JANUARY 2

All that's ahead
is in the Master's hand.
Get ready to win!

**JANUARY 3**

By working faithfully eight
hours a day, you may eventually
get to be a boss and work
twelve hours a day.

ROBERT FROST

# JANUARY 4

And we know that in
all things God works for the
good of those who love him,
who have been called
according to his purpose.

ROMANS 8:28 NIV

# JANUARY 5

Sow an act, and you reap
a habit. Sow a habit and you
reap a character. Sow a character,
and you reap a destiny.

CHARLES READE

JANUARY 6

The only place where success comes before work is in the dictionary.

# We have no more right to consume happiness without producing it, than to consume wealth without producing it.

GEORGE BERNARD SHAW

## JANUARY 8

Genius is one percent
inspiration, ninety-nine
percent perspiration.

THOMAS EDISON

JANUARY 9

So don't get tired of doing what is good. Don't get discouraged and don't give up, for we will reap a harvest of blessing at the appropriate time.

GALATIANS 6:9 NLT

# JANUARY 10

God moves in a mysterious way His wonders to perform.

WILLIAM COWPER

JANUARY 11

$\mathbf{Y}$our success
depends on you.

B. C. FORBES

JANUARY 12

Talent develops in quiet places, character in the full current of human life.

GOETHE

JANUARY 13

Courage is not simply one of the virtues but the form of every virtue at the testing point.

C. S. LEWIS

He who has begun a good
work in you will complete it
until the day of Christ Jesus.

PHILIPPIANS 1:6 NKJV

# JANUARY 15

$D$uring trying times,
keep trying!

**JANUARY 16**

You draw nothing
out of the bank of life except
what you deposit in it.

## JANUARY 17

# What would life be if we had no courage to attempt anything?

VINCENT VAN GOGH

## JANUARY 18

He who labours as
he prays lifts up his heart
to God with his hands.

BERNARD DE CLAIRVAUX

JANUARY 19

The trustworthy will get
a rich reward.  But the person
who wants to get rich quick
will only get into trouble.

PROVERBS 28:20 NLT

JANUARY 20

$A$ll experience is an arch to build upon.

HENRY ADAMS

JANUARY 21

The world is divided into people who do things and people who get the credit. Try, if you can, to belong to the first class. There's far less competition.

DWIGHT MORROW

# JANUARY 22

# We shall not be diverted from our course.

MARGARET THATCHER

## JANUARY 23

Good for the body is the work of the body, good for the soul is the work of the soul, and good for either the work of the other.

HENRY DAVID THOREAU

## JANUARY 24

I will strengthen you, Yes,
I will help you.

# JANUARY 25

Balancing your budget
is like going to heaven.
Everybody wants to do it,
but nobody wants to do what
you have to do to get there.

PHIL GRAMM

JANUARY 26

Let us work as if success depends on ourselves alone, but with the heartfelt conviction that we are doing nothing and God everything.

IGNATIUS LOYOLA

# JANUARY 27

**T**hat which we are, we are;
Made weak by time and fate,
But strong in will to strive,
To seek, to find and not to yield.

ALFRED, LORD TENNYSON

# JANUARY 28

The best way to kill an
idea is to take it to a meeting.

**JANUARY 29**

# A word spoken in due season, how good it is!

PROVERBS 15:23 KJV

JANUARY 30

It is preferable to change the world on the basis of love of mankind. But if that quality be too rare, then common sense seems the next best thing.

BESSIE HEAD

JANUARY 31

$H$e that loves God seeks neither gain nor reward but only to lose all, even himself.

JOHN OF THE CROSS

# FEBRUARY 1

We had the experience
but missed the meaning.

T. S. ELIOT

FEBRUARY 2

# Work becomes worship when done for the Lord.

## FEBRUARY 3

"**F**or I know the plans I have for you," declares the Lord, "plans to prosper you and not to harm you, plans to give you hope and a future."

JEREMIAH 29:11 NIV

# FEBRUARY 4

# I like work; it fascinates me.
I can sit and look at it for hours.

JEROME K. JEROME

# FEBRUARY 5

I long to accomplish a great and noble task; but it is my chief duty to accomplish small tasks as if they were great and noble.

HELEN KELLER

FEBRUARY 6

# Honor lies in honest toil.

GROVER CLEVELAND

FEBRUARY 7

$\mathbf{N}$obody made a greater mistake than he who did nothing because he could only do a little.

EDMUND BURKE

# FEBRUARY 8

$B$e strong and steady,
always enthusiastic for the
Lord's work, for you know
that nothing you do for the
Lord is ever useless.

1CORINTHIANS 15:58 NLT

# FEBRUARY 9

I never notice what has been done.  I only see what remains to be done.

MADAME CURIE

FEBRUARY 10

G od is a busy worker,
but He loves help.

BASQUE PROVERB

# FEBRUARY 11

Those who are quick
to promise are generally
slow to perform.

CHARLES H. SPURGEON

# FEBRUARY 12

# Nothing is particularly hard if you divide it into small jobs.

HENRY FORD

# FEBRUARY 13

Where there is no vision,
the people perish.

PROVERBS 29:18 KJV

# FEBRUARY 14

# Never wait for a miracle. Go after your dream.

JOHN C. MAXWELL

## FEBRUARY 15

You must do the thing
you think you cannot do.

ELEANOR ROOSEVELT

FEBRUARY 16

$\mathbf{I}$f we all did the things
we are capable of doing,
we would literally
astound ourselves.

Thomas Edison

**FEBRUARY 17**

Iit's surprising how
much you can accomplish
if you don't care who
gets the credit.

ABRAHAM LINCOLN

# FEBRUARY 18

# G
reater is he that is in you, than he that is in the world.

1 John 4:4 kjv

# FEBRUARY 19

God gives His gifts
where He finds the vessel
empty enough to receive them.

C. S. LEWIS

FEBRUARY 20

**W**hether you think you
can or you can't, you're right.

HENRY FORD

**FEBRUARY 21**

By perseverance the snail reached the Ark.

CHARLES H. SPURGEON

FEBRUARY 22

# Genius begins great works; labor alone finishes them.

JOSEPH JOUBERT

## FEBRUARY 23

Don't worry about anything, instead, pray about everything.

PHILIPPIANS 4:6 TLB

# FEBRUARY 24

$F$rom small beginnings
come great things.

FEBRUARY 25

All that matters is
to have faith in love
and in work, and in the
hand of God to bless both.

FEBRUARY 26

Faith will move mountains.

FEBRUARY 27

Pray to God,
but hammer away.

SPANISH PROVERB

# FEBRUARY 28

God is able to make all grace abound to you, so that in all things at all times, having all that you need, you will abound in every good work.

2 Corinthians 9:8 niv

# FEBRUARY 29

To keep a lamp burning,
we have to keep
putting oil in it.

MOTHER TERESA

# MARCH 1

You cannot be a success in any business without believing that it is the greatest business in the world....You have to put your heart in the business and the business in your heart.

THOMAS WATSON SR.

MARCH 2

The chief idea of my life is the practice of taking things with gratitude and not taking things for granted.

G. K. Chesterton

# MARCH 3

# The deed is all,
the glory nothing.

GOETHE

MARCH 4

Choose a good reputation
over great riches, for being
held in high esteem is better
than having silver and gold.

PROVERBS 22:1 NLT

MARCH 5

**T**hink before you speak
is criticism's motto; speak
before you think creation's.

E. M. FORSTER

MARCH 6

# Be great in little things.

# MARCH 7

Business, you know, may bring money, but friendship hardly ever does.

JANE AUSTEN

MARCH 8

$W$hat's a thousand dollars?
Mere chicken feed.
A poultry matter.

GROUCHO MARX

MARCH 9

Ｈis master replied,
"Well done, good and faithful
servant! You have been faithful
with a few things; I will put you
in charge of many things."

MATTHEW 25: 21 NIV

MARCH 10

The customer
is never wrong.

CESAR RITZ

MARCH 11

# **N**othing is an unmixed blessing.

HORACE

# MARCH 12

There are some times in your life when you have to call upon the best of all God gave you— and the best of what He didn't.

GLORIA NAYLOR

MARCH 13

Try first thyself, and after call in God. For to the worker God Himself lends aid.

EURPIDES

MARCH 14

# We have different gifts, according to the grace given us.

Roman 12:6 NIV

## MARCH 15

Let us with a gladsome mind
Praise the Lord, for he is kind
For his mercies endure,
Ever faithful, ever sure.

JOHN MILTON

MARCH 16

God shares with the person that is generous.

MARCH 17

# You can't build a reputation on what you are going to do.

HENRY FORD

## MARCH 18

# Women are the real architects of society.

HARRIET BEECHER STOWE

## MARCH 19

# W ork hard and cheerfully at whatever you do, as though you are working for the Lord rather than for people.

COLOSSIANS 3:23 NLT

## MARCH 20

# Two heads are better than one.

*Two are bettter than one,*

*because they have good*

*return for their work.*

<small>ECCLESIASTES 4:9 NIV</small>

# MARCH 21

If you would hit the mark,
you must aim a little above it;
Every arrow that flies feels
the attraction of earth.

LONGFELLOW

MARCH 22

The world is filled with willing
people; some willing to work,
the rest willing to let them.

ROBERT FROST

MARCH 23

**W**hatever you can do or
dream you can, begin it.
Boldness has genius, power,
and magic in it.

GOETHE

# MARCH 24

$A$ good man deals graciously and lends; He will guide his affairs with discretion.

PSALM 112:5 NKJV

MARCH 25

# Our greatest weariness comes from work not done.

ERIC HOFFER

## MARCH 26

$A$ little simplification would be the first step toward rational, I think.

ELEANOR ROOSEVELT

MARCH 27

For anything worth
having, one must pay the price;
and the price is always work,
patience, love, self-sacrifice.

JOHN BURROUGHS

MARCH 28

**F**ar and away the best prize
life offers is the chance to work
hard at work worth doing.

THEODORE ROOSEVELT

# MARCH 29

# Turn us again to yourself, O God. Make your face shine down upon us.

Psalm 80:3 NLT

## MARCH 30

It is better to wear out than rust out.

RICHARD CUMBERLAND

# MARCH 31

$D$on't forget until too
late that the business of life is
not business, but living.

B. C. FORBES

APRIL 1

$S$low but sure wins the race.

APRIL 2

W e spend our midday sweat,
    Our midnight oil;
We tire the night in thought,
    The day in toil.

FRANCIS QUARLES

APRIL 3

Always do more than
what is required of you.

JOHN WOODEN

APRIL 4

G od give me work till
my life shall end and life
til my work is done.

WINIFRED HOLTBY

APRIL 5

**N**ever be lazy in
your work, but serve
the Lord enthusiastically.

ROMANS 12:11 NLT

APRIL 6

# I'd rather be a failure
at something I love than
a success at something I hate.

GEORGE BURNS

APRIL 7

Pray with all your might
for the blessing in God, but
work at the same time with
all diligence, with all patience,
with all perseverance.
Pray, then, and work.

GEORGE MULLEER

APRIL 8

"**H**ope" is the thing
with feathers–
That perches in the soul–
And sings the tune
without the words–
And never stops—at all.

EMILY DICKINSON

APRIL 9

The difficult we do immediately. The impossible takes a little longer.

APRIL 10

$E$very spark adds to the fire.

APRIL 11

Put on tender mercies, kindness, humility, meekness, longsuffering; bearing with one another and forgiving one another.

COLOSSIANS 3:12-13 NKJV

# APRIL 12

# We are an Easter people and Alleluia is our song.

POPE JOHN PAUL II

## APRIL 13

Those who stand for
nothing fall for anything.

ALEX HAMILTON

APRIL 14

**I**f a man will begin
with certainties, he shall
end in doubts; But if he will
be content to begin with doubts,
he shall end in certainties.

FRANCIS BACON

# APRIL 15

To be, or not to be:
that is the question.

WILLIAM SHAKESPEARE

APRIL 16

$D$on't lose your head
to gain a minute,
You need your head,
Your brains are in it.

BURMA SHAVE

APRIL 17

Commit your work
to the Lord, and then
your plans will succeed.

PROVERBS 16:3 NLT

APRIL 18

People can be divided
into three groups:
Those who make things
happen, those who watch
things happen, and those
who wonder what's happening.

APRIL 19

You have to steer
your own course.

B. C. FORBES

APRIL 20

# Ideas won't work
## unless you do.

APRIL 21

Ever tried. Ever failed.
No matter. Try again.
Fail again. Fail better.

SAMUEL BECKETT

APRIL 22

Except the Lord build
the house, they labour in vain
that build it: except the Lord
keep the city, the watchman
waketh but in vain.

PSALM 127:1 KJV

APRIL 23

There are only twenty-four
hours in the day.

APRIL 24

Climb high, climb far,
your goal the sky,
your aim the star.

APRIL 25

There is no better exercise for the heart than reaching down and lifting up people.

John Andrew Holmer

# APRIL 26

$L$ife's a continuous business, and so is success, and requires continuous effort.

MARGARET THATCHER

APRIL 27

The labourer is worthy
of his hire.

LUKE 10:7 KJV

APRIL 28

$S$uccess comes in cans,
failure comes in can'ts.

APRIL 29

There are only two things to aim at in life: first, to get what you want; and after that, to enjoy it. Only the wisest of mankind achieve the second.

LOGAN PEARSALL SMITH

APRIL 30

Does the road wind
up-hill all the way?
Yes, to the very end.
Will the day's journey
take the whole long day?
From morn to night, my friend.

CHRISTINA ROSSETTI

MAY 1

R eason in man is rather
like God in the world.

THOMAS AQUINAS

MAY 2

# Through love serve one another.

GALATIANS 5:13 NKJV

# MAY 3

Be nice to people on your way up because you'll meet 'em on your way down.

## MAY 4

$H$ow can we be sold
short, or cheated, we who
for every service have
long ago been overpaid?

MEISTER ECKHART

MAY 5

Lives of great men
all remind us
we can make our lives sublime,
And, departing, leave behind us
footprints on the sands of time.

LONGFELLOW

MAY 6

# Who is narrow of vision cannot be large of heart.

CHINESE PROVERB

MAY 7

God blessed the seventh day
and made it holy, because on it
he rested from all the work of
creating he had done.

GENESIS 2:3 NIV

MAY 8

$Y$our duty, your reward,
your destiny—are here and now.

DAG HAMMARSKJOLD

MAY 9

Every Christian needs
a half hour of prayer each day,
Except when he is busy,
then he needs an hour.

FRANCIS DE SALES

MAY 10

Experience is the mother of wisdom.

## MAY 11

You can't direct the wind, but you can adjust your sails.

## MAY 12

# We must learn our limits. We are all something, but none of us are everything.

BLAISE PASCAL

## MAY 13

Let your light so shine before
men, that they may see your
good works, and glorify your
Father which is in heaven.

MATTHEW 5:16 KJV

# MAY 14

# T

hough a man be wise,
it is no shame for him
to live and learn.

SOPHOCLES

# MAY 15

Do what you can, with what you have, where you are.

THEODORE ROOSEVELT

MAY 16

A tree grows because it adds rings: a train doesn't grow by leaving one station behind and puffing on to the next.

C. S. LEWIS

MAY 17

$I$ was taught that the way of progress is neither swift nor easy.

MADAME CURIE

# MAY 18

**T**hink of ways to encourage one another to outbursts of love and good deeds.

HEBREWS 10:24 NLT

MAY 19

Good words are worth
much and cost little.

GEORGE HERBERT

MAY 20

The service we render
to others is really the rent
we pay for our room
on this earth.

MAY 21

The greatness of
work is inside man.

POPE JOHN PAUL II

MAY 22

# There is always room at the top.

DANIEL WEBSTER

## MAY 23

# He surrounds me with loving-kindness and tender mercies. He fills my life with good things!

PSALM 103:4-5 TLB

# MAY 24

Little ponds never
hold big fish.

MAY 25

Free men freely work:
whoever fears God fears
to sit at ease.

ELIZABETH BARRETT BROWNING

MAY 26

O Lord, let us not live to be useless, for Christ's sake.

JOHN WESLEY

MAY 27

Truth is like life; it has to be taken in its entirety or not at all. Isolated truths will not do.

FULTON SHEEN

MAY 28

In union there is strength.

MAY 29

For just as the body without the spirit is dead, so faith without works is also dead.

JAMES 2:26 NRSV

MAY 30

# When one door shuts, another opens.

## MAY 31

Your character is your
own handiwork.

B. C. FORBES

# JUNE 1

Do you think the work God gives us to do is never easy? Jesus says His yoke is easy, His burden is light. People sometimes refuse to do God's work just because it is easy. This is sometimes because they cannot believe that easy work is His work.

GEORGE MACDONALD

JUNE 2

# Work expands to fit the time available.

PARKINSON'S LAW

# JUNE 3

**M**ake the best use of what is in your power, and take the rest as it happens.

EPICTETUS

JUNE 4

If any of you lacks wisdom,
let him ask of God, who gives
to all liberally and without
reproach, and it will
be given to him.

JAMES 1:5 NKJV

# JUNE 5

Footprints in the sands
of time are not made
by sitting down.

## JUNE 6

Lord, grant that I may always desire more than I can accomplish.

MICHELANGELO

JUNE 7

$T$o be trusted is a greater
compliment than to be loved.

GEORGE MACDONALD

JUNE 8

Thinking is the talking
of the soul with itself.

PLATO

JUNE 9

$P$eople may think they are
doing what is right, but the
Lord examines the heart.

Proverbs 21:2 nlt

JUNE 10

# First impressions
are the most lasting.

## JUNE 11

$Y$ou can become the person
you have always wanted to be.

ROBERT SCHULLER

JUNE 12

# Winning isn't everything, but wanting to win is.

VINCE LOMBARDI

## JUNE 13

Character cannot be developed in ease and quiet. Only through experience of trial and suffering can the soul be strengthened, vision cleared, ambition inspired, and success achieved.

HELEN KELLER

JUNE 14

$I$ will never leave you
or forsake you.

HEBREWS 13:5 NRSV

JUNE 15

Everyone should carefully observe which way his heart draws him, and then choose that way with all his strength.

JUNE 16

$N$othing is so strong as
gentleness, nothing so
gentle as real strength.

<small>Francis de Sales</small>

# JUNE 17

# Here stand I. I can do no other. God help me. Amen.

MARTIN LUTHER

JUNE 18

Determination —
Thought shall be the harder,
heart the keener, courage the
greater, as our might lessens.

JUNE 19

**F**or wisdom will enter your heart, and knowledge will be pleasant to your soul. Discretion will protect you, and understanding will guard you.

PROVERBS 2:10-11 NIV

JUNE 20

$P$urpose has to do with one's calling-deciding what business you are in as a person.

KEN BLANCHARD/NORMAN VINCENT PEALE

JUNE 21

I t is often just as sacred
to laugh as it is to pray.

CHARLES SWINDOLL

JUNE 22

Settle yourself in solitude
and you will come upon
Him in yourself.

JUNE 23

No pessimist ever discovered
the secrets of the stars, or sailed
to an uncharted land,
or opened a new heaven
to the human spirit.

HELEN KELLER

JUNE 24

Now faith is the substance of things hoped for, the evidence of things not seen.

HEBREWS 11:1 KJV

# JUNE 25

Only those who will risk going too far can possibly find out how far one can go.

T. S. ELIOT

JUNE 26

# Even if you're on the right track, you'll get run over if you just sit there.

WILL ROGERS

## JUNE 27

$A$lways aim for
achievement and
forget about success.

HELEN HAYES

JUNE 28

# When one must, one can.

YIDDISH PROVERB

## JUNE 29

$W$e are judged by what we finish, not by what we start.

JUNE 30

The desire accomplished
is sweet to the soul.

JOEL 13:19 NIV

JULY 1

You may have to fight a battle

more than once to win it.

MARGARET THATCHER

JULY 2

Be simple; take our Lord's
hand and walk through things.

FATHER. ANDREW

JULY 3

Great works do not always
lie in our way, but every moment
we may do little ones excellently,
that is, with great love.

FRANCIS DE SALES

JULY 4

Self-discipline never means giving up everything, for giving up is a loss. Our Lord did not ask us to give up the things of earth, but to exchange them for better things.

FULTON SHEEN

JULY 5

Labor not for the food which perishes, but for that food which endures to everlasting life, which the Son of man shall give to you.

JOHN 6:27 NIV

## JULY 6

He who lives only
for himself is truly
dead to others.

PUBLILIUS SYRUS

JULY 7

# Nothing is as easy as it looks.

MURPHY'S LAW

JULY 8

# When you cease to make a contribution, you begin to die.

ELEANOR ROOSEVELT

## JULY 9

**W**e may think God
wants actions of a certain
kind, but God wants
people of a certain kind.

C. S. LEWIS

JULY 10

# Whoever gives heed to instruction prospers, and blessed is he who trusts in the Lord.

PROVERBS 16:20 NIV

## JULY 11

Life is an exciting
business, and it is most
exciting when it is
lived for others.

HELEN KELLER

JULY 12

A faithful and good
servant is a real godsend;
but truly it is a rare
bird in the land.

MARTIN LUTHER

JULY 13

$U$nless we perform
divine service with every
willing act of our life,
we never perform it at all.

JOHN RUSKIN

JULY 14

$I$t is better to be poor
and honest than to be
a fool and dishonest.

PROVERBS 19:1 NLT

# JULY 15

Do little things as though they were great, because of the majesty of Jesus Christ who does them in us.

BLAISE PASCAL

JULY 16

What lies in our power
to do, it lies in our
power not to do.

ARISTOTLE

JULY 17

So I decided there is nothing better than to enjoy food and drink and to find satisfaction in work. Then I realized that this pleasure is from the hand of God.

ECCLESIASTES 2:24 NLT

JULY 18

Behold the turtle.
He makes progress only
when he sticks his neck out.

JULY 19

Three things are necessary for the salvation of man: to know what he ought to believe; to know what he ought to desire; and to know what he ought to do.

THOMAS AQUINAS

# JULY 20

But those who hope in the Lord will renew their strength. They will soar on wings like eagles; they will run and not grow weary, they will walk and not be faint.

ISAIAH 40:31 NIV

JULY 21

A mistake is simply another way of doing things.

KATHERINE GRAHAM

JULY 22

I know God won't give me anything I can't handle. I just wish He didn't trust me so much.

MOTHER TERESA

JULY 23

$A$ll God's giants have been weak men, who did great things for God because they believed that God would be with them.

HUDSON TAYLOR

JULY 24

To do thy will is more than praise,
As words are less than deeds;
And simple trust can find thy ways,
We miss with chart of creeds.

J. G. WHITTIER

# JULY 25

# He conquers who overcomes himself.

LATIN PROVERB

## JULY 26

Therefore do not worry
about tomorrow, for tomorrow
will worry about itself.
Each day has enough
trouble of its own.

MATTHEW 6:34 NIV

# JULY 27

There are so many men who can figure costs, and so few who can measure values.

CALIFORNIA TRIBUNE

JULY 28

Vision that looks inward becomes duty. Vision that looks outward becomes aspiration. Vision that looks upward becomes faith.

JULY 29

There are diversities of gifts,
but the same Spirit.

1 Corinthians 12:4 nkjv

JULY 30

A good life is the
best sermon.

JULY 31

It takes as much courage to have tried and failed, as it does to have tried and succeeded.

<small>ANNE MORROW LINDBERGH</small>

# AUGUST 1

$A$nd so, since God
in his mercy has given us
this wonderful ministry,
we never give up.

2 CORINTHIANS 4:1 NLT

# AUGUST 2

Defeat is temporary;
giving up is permanent.

AUGUST 3

Pleasure in the job puts
perfection in the work.

ARISTOTLE

AUGUST 4

# Success is never final.

WINSTON CHURCHILL

## AUGUST 5

Faithfulness is the measure of success.

CHUCK COLSON

AUGUST 6

Don't copy the behavior
and customs of this world,
but let God transform you
into a new person by changing
the way you think.

ROMANS 12:2 NLT

AUGUST 7

Coming together is a beginning; keeping together is progress; working together is success.

HENRY FORD

AUGUST 8

Nothing is ever done beautifully which is done in rivalship, nor nobly which is done in pride.

JOHN RUSKIN

# AUGUST 9

The "wages" of every noble
work do yet lie in Heaven
or else nowhere.

Thomas Carlyle

## AUGUST 10

The secret of joy in work is contained in one word—excellence. To know how to do something well is to enjoy it.

PEARL S. BUCK

# AUGUST 11

I can't imagine a
person becoming a success
who doesn't give the game of
life everything he's got.

WALTER CRONKITE

# AUGUST 12

$I$ have come that they
may have life, and that they
may have it more abundantly.

JOHN 10:10 NKJV

AUGUST 13

Success is more
attitude than aptitude.

AUGUST 14

$A$bsence of occupation is
not rest, a mind quite vacant
is a mind distress'd.

WILLIAM COWPER

# AUGUST 15

$I$f at first you do succeed,
try something harder.

## AUGUST 16

$I$t is not your business
to succeed, but to do right:
when you have done so,
the rest lies with God.

C. S. LEWIS

# AUGUST 17

Βut the wisdom that
comes from heaven is first
of all pure. It is also peace
loving, gentle at all times, and
willing to yield to others.
It is full of mercy and
good deeds.

JAMES 3:17 NLT

# AUGUST 18

$S$uccess is counted sweetest
By those who ne'er succeed.
To comprehend a nectar
Requires sorest need.

EMILY DICKINSON

AUGUST 19

I know of no case where a man added to his dignity by standing on it.

Winston Churchill

AUGUST 20

The purest treasure
mortal times afford is
a spotless reputation.

WILLIAM SHAKESPEARE

AUGUST 21

It's a recession when
your neighbor loses his job;
it's a depression when
you lose yours.

HARRY TRUMAN

# AUGUST 22

$\mathbf{I}$f God be for us,
who can be against us?

ROMANS 8:31 NIV

AUGUST 23

Don't seek the blessing,
seek the blesser.

AUGUST 24

# He who ceases to pray, ceases to prosper.

WILLIAM GURNEY BENHAM

# AUGUST 25

I do not pray for a
lighter load, but for
a stronger back.

PHILLIPS BROOKS

# AUGUST 26

Learn to take your every
problem to the Bible.
Within its pages you
will find the correct answer.

BILLY GRAHAM

AUGUST 27

When you find yourself
in a hole, stop digging.

ULYSSES S. GRANT

AUGUST 28

Aspire to lead a quiet life, to mind your own business, and to work with your hands.

1 Thessalonians 4:11 NKJV

AUGUST 29

Never put off until
tomorrow what you
can put off indefinitely.

## AUGUST 30

$G$od has promised forgiveness
to your repentance, but He has
not promised tomorrow
to your procrastination.

AUGUSTINE

AUGUST 31

To talk much and
arrive nowhere is the
same as climbing a
tree to catch a fish.

CHINESE PROVERB

# SEPTEMBER 1

# Where God guides, He provides.

## SEPTEMBER 2

Better is a handful with quietness, than both the hands full with toil and a chasing after the wind.

ECCLESIASTES 4:6 NIV

SEPTEMBER 3

$G$od sees every one
of us; He creates every
soul...for a purpose.

<small>JOHN HENRY NEWMAN</small>

# SEPTEMBER 4

A prudent question
is one half of wisdom.

<small>Francis Bacon</small>

# SEPTEMBER 5

# The Almighty has His own purposes.

ABRAHAM LINCOLN

# SEPTEMBER 6

# Leave results to God.

ELIZABETH BARRETT BROWNING

# SEPTEMBER 7

A good name is better than precious ointment.

ECCLESIASTES 7:1 KJV

# SEPTEMBER 8

My hope is built on
nothing less
Than Jesus' blood
and righteousness.

EDWARD MOTE

SEPTEMBER 9

**M**ore things are wrought by prayer, than this world dreams of.

ALFRED, LORD TENNYSON

# SEPTEMBER 10

# Well begun is half done.

ENGLISH PROVERB

# SEPTEMBER 11

# We walk by faith, not by sight.

2 CORINTHIANS 5:7 NIV

# SEPTEMBER 12

The best prayers have often
more groans than words.

**SEPTEMBER 13**

God never imposes a duty
without giving time to do it.

JOHN RUSKIN

SEPTEMBER 14

The perpetual hurry of business and company ruins me in soul if not in body.

WILLIAM WILBERFORCE

SEPTEMBER 15

If you work on behalf of the hungry and satisfy the afflicted, then shall your light rise in the darkness, and your night shall be as the noonday.

ISAIAH 58:10 NIV

SEPTEMBER 16

The next thing to being wise oneself is to live in a circle of those who are wise.

C. S. Lewis

# SEPTEMBER 17

God doesn't call the equipped, He equips the called.

**SEPTEMBER 18**

You should keep a clear
mind in every situation.

2 TIMOTHY 4:5 NLT

# SEPTEMBER 19

# All service ranks the same with God.

ROBERT BROWNING

# SEPTEMBER 20

# Poverty is no sin.

## SEPTEMBER 21

It's not how many hours you put in but how much you put into the hours.

**SEPTEMBER 22**

Most high, glorious God,
enlighten the darkness of
my heart and give me, Lord,
a correct faith, a certain hope,
a perfect charity, sense of
knowledge, so that I may
carry out Your holy and
true command.

FRANCIS OF ASSISI

## SEPTEMBER 23

Give God thy heart, thy
service and thy gold;
The day wears on and
time is waxing old.

SUNDIAL INSCRIPTION

# SEPTEMBER 24

Y ou know the grace of our Lord Jesus Christ, that, though he was rich, yet for your sakes he became poor, that you through his poverty might be rich.

2 Corinthians 8:9 niv

# SEPTEMBER 25

$\text{I}$ find the doing of the will
of God leaves me no time
for disputing about His plans.

GEORGE MACDONALD

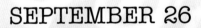

SEPTEMBER 26

If you can learn to laugh in spite of the circumstances that surround you, you will enrich others, enrich yourself, and more than that, you will last!

BARBARA JOHNSON

# SEPTEMBER 27

Tact is the art of
making a point without
making an enemy.

# SEPTEMBER 28

Use your gifts faithfully,
and they shall be enlarged;
practice what you know,
and you shall attain to
higher knowledge.

MATTHEW ARNOLD

SEPTEMBER 29

Your talent is God's gift to you.
What you do with it is
your gift back to God.

LEO BUSCAGLIA

# SEPTEMBER 30

The Kingdom of Heaven is like a pearl merchant on the lookout for choice pearls. When he discovered a pearl of great value, he sold everything he owned and bought it!

MATTHEW 13:45 NLT

# OCTOBER 1

All our talents increase
in the using, and every
faculty, both good and bad,
strengthens by exercise.

ANNE BRONTE

OCTOBER 2

Today is a gift. That's why it's called the present.

OCTOBER 3

A Christian is a person who thinks in believing and believes in thinking.

AUGUSTINE

OCTOBER 4

Change your thoughts and
you change your world.

NORMAN VINCENT PEALE

OCTOBER 5

The one who has God
for his treasure has all
things in one.

A. W. TOZER

OCTOBER 6

The steadfast love of
the Lord never ceases,
His mercies never come
to an end; they are new
every morning; great
is your faithfulness.

LAMENTATIONS 3:22-23 NRSV

# OCTOBER 7

Trust the past to God's mercy, the present to God's love and the future to God's providence.

AUGUSTINE

OCTOBER 8

The very vastness of the work raises one's thoughts to God, as the only one by whom it can be done. That is the solid comfort—He knows!

FLORENCE NIGHTINGALE

# OCTOBER 9

# We may easily be too big for God to use, but never too small.

D. L. MOODY

OCTOBER 10

Good keeps His holy mysteries just on the outside of man's dream.

ELIZABETH BARRETT BROWNING

OCTOBER 11

Every mother is a working mother.

**OCTOBER 12**

See, my servant will
act wisely, he will be
raised and lifted up
and highly exalted.

ISAIAH 52:13 NIV

# OCTOBER 13

Two works of mercy
set a man free: forgive and
you will be forgiven, and give
and you will receive.

OCTOBER 14

$I$t will do us good to
be very empty, to be very weak,
to be very distrustful of self,
and so to go about our
Master's work.

C. H. Spurgeon

# OCTOBER 15

If you want to feel rich, just count all the things you have that money can't buy.

Gold can no more fill the spirit of a man, than grace his purse. A man may as well fill a bag with wisdom, as the soul with the world.

ROBERT BOLTON

# OCTOBER 17

God helping you: Take your everyday, ordinary life—your sleeping, eating, going-to-work, and walking-around life—and place it before God as an offering. Embracing what God does for you is the best thing you can do for him.

ROMANS 12:1 THE MESSAGE

# OCTOBER 18

There is nothing wrong
with people possessing riches.
The wrong comes when riches
possess people.

BILLY GRAHAM

OCTOBER 19

An ounce of will-power
is worth a pound of learning.

OCTOBER 20

There is a net of love
by which you can catch souls.

MOTHER TERESA

OCTOBER 21

There is a grace of kind listening as well as a grace of kind speaking.

**OCTOBER 22**

If you cannot be a Christian
where you are, you cannot be a
Christian anywhere.

HENRY WARD BEECHER

# OCTOBER 23

If God can work through me,
He can work through anyone.

FRANCIS OF ASSISI

# OCTOBER 24

Let me burn out for God.

HENRY MARTYN

OCTOBER 25

Live your beliefs and you
can turn the world around.

HENRY DAVID THOREAU

OCTOBER 26

If you have not the Spirit of God, Christian worker, remember that you stand in somebody else's way; you are a fruitless tree standing where a fruitful tree might grow.

C. H. SPURGEON

# OCTOBER 27

$S$uit the action to the word,
the word to the action.

SHAKESPEARE

OCTOBER 28

But the fruit of the Spirit
is love, joy, peace, patience,
kindness, goodness, faithfulness,
gentleness and self-control.

GALATIANS 5:22 NIV

OCTOBER 29

# Joy is the serious business of heaven.

OCTOBER 30

Let us not cease to do the utmost, that we may incessantly go forward in the way of the Lord; and let us not despair of the smallness of our accomplishments.

JOHN CALVIN

# OCTOBER 31

If you do not wish
God's kingdom, don't pray
for it. But if you do, you
must do more than pray
for it; you must work for it.

JOHN RUSKIN

NOVEMBER 1

An ant on the move does
more than a dozing ox.

NOVEMBER 2

Do not be anxious about anything, but in everything, by prayer and petition, with thanksgiving, present your requests to God.

PHILIPPIANS 4:6 NIV

# NOVEMBER 3

Do all the good you can
By all the means you can
In all the ways you can
In all the places you can
To all the people you can
As long as you ever can.

JOHN WESLEY

# NOVEMBER 4

For the Christian, this world is an arena, not an armchair.

NOVEMBER 5

If you keep in step with God, you'll be out of step with the world.

NOVEMBER 6

# Our work here is brief but its reward is eternal.

CLARE OF ASSISI

## NOVEMBER 7

For I can do everything with
the help of Christ who gives
me the strength I need.

PHILIPPIANS 4:13 NLT

# NOVEMBER 8

$T$oday is the tomorrow we worried about yesterday.

**NOVEMBER 9**

Find some work for your hands to do, so that Satan may never find you idle.

JEROME

# NOVEMBER 10

The salvation of
human souls is the
real business of life.

C. S. LEWIS

NOVEMBER 11

**W**alk so close
to God that nothing
can come between you.

# NOVEMBER 12

$O$ur job is not
to straighten each other out,
but to help each other up.

NEVA COYLE

# NOVEMBER 13

Whatever is true, whatever is noble, whatever is right, whatever is pure, whatever is lovely, whatever is admirable—if anything is excellent or praiseworthy—think about such things.

PHILIPPIANS 4:8 NIV

# NOVEMBER 14

The first test of a really great man is his humility.

JOHN RUSKIN

# NOVEMBER 15

Never talk defeat.
Use words like hope,
belief, faith, victory.

NORMAN VINCENT PEALE

# NOVEMBER 16

Our only business is to love
and delight ourselves in God.

BROTHER LAWRENCE

NOVEMBER 17

No matter how low you feel, if you count your blessings, you'll always show a profit.

## NOVEMBER 18

Let not your hands
be weak: for your work
shall be rewarded.

2 Chronicles 15:7 kjv

# NOVEMBER 19

Beware lest you lose
the substance by grasping
at the shadow.

AESOP

# NOVEMBER 20

O urs is more than mental work; it is heart work—the labor of the inmost soul.

C. H. SPURGEON

# NOVEMBER 21

**D**etermination
Effort
Sacrifice
Initiative
Responsibility
Enthusiasm

# NOVEMBER 22

# W e must accept finite disappointment, but we must never lose infinite hope.

MARTIN LUTHER KING JR.

# NOVEMBER 23

This is the day the Lord
has made; let us rejoice
and be glad in it.

PSALM 118:24  NIV

# NOVEMBER 24

O Lord, you give us everything, at the price of an effort.

LEONARDO DAVINCI

NOVEMBER 25

M ost of the important
things in the world have been
accomplished by people
who have kept on trying
where there seemed
to be no hope at all.

DALE CARNEGIE

NOVEMBER 26

Thank the Lord for his
steadfast love, for his
wonderful works to humankind.
for he satisfies the thirsty,
and the hungry he fills
with good things.

PSALM 107:8-9 NRSV

# NOVEMBER 27

Don't let life discourage you; everyone who got where he is had to begin where he was.

RICHARD L. EVANS

# NOVEMBER 28

$N$ever give in, never give in, never, never, never, never— In nothing, great or small, large or petty—never give in except to convictions of honor and good sense.

WINSTON CHURCHILL

# NOVEMBER 29

**W**hatever you do,
whether in word or deed,
do it all in the name of the
Lord Jesus,giving thanks to God
the Father through him.

COLOSSIANS 3:17 NIV

# NOVEMBER 30

$O$ptimism means faith in men, in the human potential; hope means faith in God and in His omnipotence.

Carlo Carretto

# DECEMBER 1

To become what we
are capable of becoming
is the only end in life.

ROBERT LEWIS STEVENSON

# DECEMBER 2

Every job is a self-portrait
of the person who did it.
Autograph your work
with excellence.

# DECEMBER 3

$I$t is not fair to ask of others what you are unwilling to do yourself.

ELEANOR ROOSEVELT

# DECEMBER 4

# Walk worthy of the Lord.

COLOSSIANS 1:10 KJV

# DECEMBER 5

An expert is someone
who has made all the
mistakes which can be
made, in a narrow field.

NIELS BOHR

# DECEMBER 6

Learn from the mistakes
of others. You can't live
long enough to make
them all yourself.

# DECEMBER 7

It is nobler to try something and fail than to try nothing and succeed. The result may be the same, but you won't be. We always grow more through defeats than victories.

DECEMBER 8

Removing all risks from your life renders faith unnecessary. Faith requires risks!

KEN MAHAYNES

# DECEMBER 9

# God's strong hand is on you; he'll promote you at the right time.

1 PETER 5:6-7 THE MESSAGE

# DECEMBER 10

# Holiness consists of doing the will of God with a smile.

MOTHER TERESA

# DECEMBER 11

All the works mentioned throughout the Bible are written up as works of faith.

MARTIN LUTHER

DECEMBER 12

A quiet morning with a
loving God puts the events
of the upcoming day into
proper perspective.

JANETTE OKE

# DECEMBER 13

I learned to practice mustard seed faith, and positive thinking, and remarkable things happened.

SIR JOHN WALTON

# DECEMBER 14

The saints of God are sealed inwardly with faith, but outwardly with good works.

JOHN BOYS

DECEMBER 15

The Lord bless you and
keep you; the Lord make
his face shine upon you and
be gracious to you; the Lord
turn his face toward
you and give you peace.

NUMBERS 6:24-26 NIV

# DECEMBER 16

The trouble with learning from experience is that you never graduate.

DECEMBER 17

$F$aithfulness in carrying out present duties is the best preparation for the future.

FRANCOIS FENELON

# DECEMBER 18

# He does most in God's great world, who does his best in his own little world.

THOMAS JEFFERSON

# DECEMBER 19

H e that has a head
of wax must not walk
in the sun.

GEORGE HERBERT

DECEMBER 20

# God did not call us to be successful, but to be faithful.

MOTHER TERESA

# DECEMBER 21

Y̲ou have nothing to
do in life except to live
in union with Christ.

RUFUS MOSELY

DECEMBER 22

Christians are the only people
in the world who have anything
to be happy about.

BILLY GRAHAM

DECEMBER 23

I will honor Christmas
in my heart, and try to
keep it all the year.

CHARLES DICKENS

DECEMBER 24

For to us a child is born, to us a son is given, and the government will be on his shoulders. and he will be called Wonderful, Counselor, Mighty God, Everlasting Father, Prince of Peace.

ISAIAH 9:6 NIV

# DECEMBER 25

If the work of God could be comprehended by reason, it would be no longer wonderful, and faith would have no merit if reason provided proof.

GREGORY THE GREAT

# DECEMBER 26

When all is said and done, there is usually more said than done.

DECEMBER 27

Thou shalt ever joy at
eventide if you spend
the day fruitfully.

THOMAS À KEMPIS

# DECEMBER 28

$G$ive generously, for
your gifts will return
to you later.

ECCLESIASTES 11:1 TLB

DECEMBER 29

It is well to think well;
it is Divine to act well.

HORACE MANN

# DECEMBER 30

$\mathrm{I}$ know of only one
duty, and that is to love.

CAMUS

# DECEMBER 31